At the Hive Entrance
by H. STORCH

At the Hive Entrance
by H. STORCH

OBSERVATION HANDBOOK

"How to know what happens inside the hive by observation on the outside".

EUROPEAN APICULTURAL EDITIONS
EUROPESE BIJENTEELT UITGAVEN
EDITIONS EUROPEENNES APICOLES
EUROPÄISCHE BIENENZUCHT AUSGABEN

B-1040 BRUSSEL, 1, rue de l'Escadron

AT THE HIVE ENTRANCE
by H. Storch

This book was published in German under the title:
"Am Flugloch".

Translation: F. Celis.

D/1566/1985/1

© All copyrights and translation rights strictly reserved for all countries included U.S.S.R.

When preparing this first edition, we asked Dr. DREHER, who collaborated with Prof. STORCH, to revise the text, paying particular attention to the latest developments in the field of bees disease, and we want to thank him warmly for this.

We have also thought it useful to complete the observations made at the hive entrance and on the bottom board cover, with those interesting observations that one can make at the building frame and which we have taken from the book »Der Baurahmen« written by the inventor and promotor M.E. PASCHKE.

So it is that we can present our readers with a set of observations, all of which can be made by the beekeeper without him having to open or work within the colony.
All these observations are very interesting, but only useful if they are understood and correctly interpreted.

This is the aim of this work.

The editor.

Contents.

	Preface	5
A.	During the Winter	7
B.	The Day of the Cleansing Flight	15
C.	Spring	21
D.	The Main Period of flowering	
	1. May	30
	2. June	32
	3. July	40
E.	Preparing for the Winter	
	1. August	49
	2. September	53
	3. October	54
	4. November	58
F.	The Winter Bottom Board Cover	60
G.	The Building Frame	63
	Conclusions	67

Preface.

All year round it is through this little opening that the life of a colony pulses. Here it breathes and rejects all that it will not tolerate in its domain. Here it transmits its meaningful message for the person who can understand it. Here the colony's behaviour informs the beekeeper of its problems and state of health, and lets him know whether it needs his help.

A keeper who can tell the condition of his bees by observing the hive entrance does not need to open his hives and disturb the bees' sanctuary, the brood nest. This never produces good results.

A healthy colony must have peace if it is to perform its productive role. On principle a visit should only be made once the keeper has determined at the hive entrance that something is not in order. It is not always easy to know what is happening inside the hive by observing the hive entrance and this is only learnt after many years, especially when the keeper is alone and there is no-one to give advice.

The aquisition of this knowledge can be facilitated by complementing observations at the hive entrance with those made at the rear window or at the building frame. A look beneath the frames is also very often instructive.

As long as the beekeeper cannot understand the internal condition of the hive by watching the outside, he can only lose money and will have to pay his apprenticeship dearly.

Therefore it is in the best interest of every beekeeper to learn this field as fast and as thoroughly as possible. It is not only the ears and eyes of the observer which must participate, but also his senses of smell and touch, and above all his heart, spirit and intelligence.

I feel I had to write this book because, to my knowledge, there is no similar existing work and, besides, in my position as teacher of apiculture and as a master-beekeeper, I have often noticed a lack of explanations in this area. Starting from a specific observation, I have tried to draw the appropriate conclusion and to clarify in this way the causes and effects of all that happens within the hive.

A. During the Winter.

Observation	Explanation
Any beekeeper worth the name has to know what is taking place within the hive during the course of the winter months. On a quiet day, listen at the entrance of a well-populated hive which has no intermediate bottom board. Most people will not hear anything at all; but a well trained ear will distinguish a soft buzz, similar to a lightly uttered "sh".	Colonies which behave like this are healthy and are wintering perfectly. In such colony the cluster together with the queen fills the empty cells where the previous brood emerged. The average temperature of this area is close to 25°C. On the edge of the cluster the temperature is halved (after Dr. Büdel + 10°C). (A continuous to and fro movement from the outside to the center of the cluster occurs; the older bees are to be found on the outside). One believes this "circulation" to be the cause of the observed soft buzz. Mortality in such populations is always very low.
Listen at the hive entrance in the same manner. One observes a few solitary bees flying away and the snow in front of the hive is soiled with faeces.	This time the noise will be more pronounced, as if one whispered st or zs - zr. The noise originates from bees that are sick or in need of relief. As this noise is often heard around the hive entrance one can assume that these bees have already moved away from the cluster. Such hives are not wintering well and one often find a large number of dead bees on the bottom board.
If one listens at the hive entrance on a day when the temperature has sharply increased or decreased, one can hear a buzz resembling an evening breeze in a forest.	As the temperature increases, the winter cluster breaks apart; if it decreases rapidly the bees draw closer together. The buzz heard is a result of these movements. It is difficult to establish whether there has been an increase in respiratory activity in both cases. The experienced beekeeper is always woried by sharp changes in temperature during the winter and between day and night as they always involve an increased consumption of food.

Observation	Explanation
Anyone listening at the hive entrance will notice how the bees react with a louder buzz to someone walking heavily on the hive floor, the wind slamming the door shut, a snowball being thrown onto the roof etc.	All these noises are abnormal occurences. The bangs and vibrations spread through and affect the drowsy wintering populations; they always cause an increase in food consumption. On the other hand a colony easily adapts itself to a regularly repeated disturbance, for example, passing trains, lorries, cars. All the above mentioned observations are more easily heard when a listening tube is used.
If a beekeeper leaves the hive entrance unprotected during the winter,	he is definitely ignoring the detrimental consequences that his carelessness may entail. The strong winds of Autumn and Winter, which may last uninterrupted for several days, can easily reach the colony. In this case, using a listening tube, one can easily determine how badly the colony's winter rest has been disturbed. At such times many bees stray from the protective cluster, they get lost in the empty spaces where they become drowsy and die hanging onto the frames or fall onto the floor of the hive. Proof is found on the day of the cleansing flight. There will be many more dead bees on the bottom board of hives with an unprotected entrance than on those which have either an intermediate bottom board, porch or protective hall. It is thus clear that disturbances arising from winds or storms result in an increased consumption of food reserves, and that the slightest ray of winter sun may even attract the odd bee out into the open. The beekeeper who has no other means of protection at his disposal can simply place a tile, heavy enough to resist winds, over the hive entrance.
Isolated bees flying away, brown faeces at the hive entrance, on the alighting board or on the snow near the hive.	This is a sign of dysentery which can have different origins: unclean winter food stores, too cold a hive, serious disturbances provoked by bad weather, queenlessness, disease (nosema, acarine, mite). It is advisable to induce a cleansing flight by administering warm liquid nourishment at mid-day as soon as the temperature reaches 5 to 7° C. Colonies at the edge of the hive whose flanks are not well enough protected, those which are wintering on

Observation	Explanation
	immature combs or those which are too weak and too cold are more prone to dysentry. They have to consume more food in order to maintain their vital temperature. Bees which only have to defecate a little are surviving the winter best.
Scraps of combs are found at the hive entrance. Simultaneously signs of dysentery may be observed.	A mouse has made its nest in the hive (this occurs mostly in straw hives or in those with too large an entrance).
Dead bees, nibbled or torn to pieces lie strewn at the hive entrance.	A shrew has disturbed the cluster (the hive entrance is higher than 6 mm.) It must be chased away and the height of the entrance must be reduced, otherwise it will continue to feed on the bees which stray from the irritated cluster.
A badly soiled hive entrance gives off heat and spreads an odour resembling that of fresh bread.	The colony has dysentery. I have known this to happen as early as New Year if the beekeeper was careless or untrained. Such a situation will occur particularly early when a colony has only honeydew to feed on. It leaves more indigestible waste which soon overloads the intestines of the bees. Because of the cold weather, always frequent at this time of the year, the bees are unable to relieve themselves outside. First they defecate near the hive entrance then on the side walls, roof, frames and lastly the honeycomb. The colony tries to keep this clean as long as possible. Finally they defecate on each other. The colony can no longer be saved at this stage for nosema also creates havoc. And yet, such catastrophes can easily be avoided by a well-informed beekeeper.
Passing in front of the hives in the middle of winter one hears a continuous buzzing from one colony.	This buzz is not necessarily due to queenlessness. It is sometimes sufficient to enlarge the hive entrance, which may have been too small, and remove with a

Observation	Explanation
	metal hook dead bees and wax clots. When calm slowly returns and when on the following day the buzzing has ceased, the reason was that the colony had been suffering from a lack of oxygen. It appears from questions put each spring to the apicultural research center in Marburg, that in Hessen (Germany) alone, each year a large number of colonies die of "suffocation". Experience shows that usually the stronger populations perish from such carelessness.
Ice crystals are seen at the hive entrance.	This only occurs in very cold weather and is usually observed in hives with low frames rather than high ones. The greater the number of bees, the larger the cluster of crystals. It is due to the water-vapour released in the bees breath crystallizing as ice. It has been possible to conclude from the absence of crystals that several colonies in an apiary located in the Erzgebirge, when the outdoor temperature was $-25°$ C (1938-1939), had already died at the beginning of February. The bees had consumed all the readily available food and due to the extreme cold had been unable to move to the frames where stocks were kept.
The hive entrances are completely blocked with snow.	As long as the snow remains powdery it is not airtight and the bees breathing is therefore not seriously hampered. But as soon as it begins to melt and threatens to freeze over-night there is a risk of it blocking the hive-entrance and it is thus advisable to remove it.
Dead bees are found, even during the winter, between the hive entrance and the raised alighting board.	This occurs particularly in well-populated hives and there are no reasons for concern. The bees always endeavour to keep the bottom board of the hive as clean as possible, and in order to do so carry their dead to this more or less obscure area as they do not yet want to risk venturing outside to get rid of them. These dead bees must be removed in order to allow fresh air to circulate freely.

Observation	Explanation
Scraps of wood and other damage are found at one or more hive entrances.	A woodpecker is at work and searching for food. If it succeeded at its first attempt it will certainly return. The violent pecking so seriously upsets the colony that the bees go to the hive entrance where the woodpecker eats them. It will no only peck at the hive entrance but also at the front wall and, in the case of straw hives tear away tufts of straw with its strong beak. The bees which get eaten are the least of the damage, more serious in the high consumption of food and the ensuing dysentery. The following is a brief true exemple. A beekeeper had 6 colonies in straw hives located behind his barn. Troughout the winter he never went past the area. When he felt it was the time for the cleansing flight he visited the apiary only to find the populations dead. The hives were dislodged and pierced up to the combs; two wood-peckers were still in the vicinity. (If a fence of strong, narrowly spaced wires is placed around the hives, not only wood-peckers but other birds are kept at a distance).
When it becomes warmer after a period of extreme cold, water is found at the hive entrance, particularly when the hive contains a vigorous colony.	From all the questions asked, notably after the drastic month of February 1956, it seems that this observation puzzles many beekeepers. There is however no reason for concern, for on the contrary, the observation indicates a promising colony. During the winter months each cluster warms only itself and not the whole of the surrounding hive. As is known, heating implies food consumption. Bees continuously exhale water vapour, some of which escapes through the hive entrance and the rest settles on the hive walls where, in times of frost, it freezes and crystallizes and so the bees population finds itself living in a "palace of ice". As it becomes warmer, the ice melts and water trickles on the bottom board to appear soon at the hive entrance. Experience shows that strong, healthy colonies that have spent the winter in good conditions and were not disturbed come to no harm in even the most severe cold weather. Only vigorous populations with a early brood are an exception.

Photograph 1

Drone larvae

After a period of cold or one without harvest at the end of April or beginning of May, it is not unusual to see bees ejecting drones at the hive entrance. They also suck the food from those cells which have contained drone larvae as it is pointless to feed them. The same thing happens in August when the drones are expelled.

Photograph 2

Pollen loss

When the hive entrance is too narrow or its ridges too sharp, the bees often lose the pollen-loads they have so laboriously collected in hazardous conditions. Each hive entrance should be equipped with a device enabling its height and width to be altered depending on the season and strength of the colony.

B. The day of the Cleansing Flight.

As soon as the cleansing flight has begun, all waste-matter must be removed from the bottom-board. Observations made at this time will supply much information that will complete information gained at the hive entrance. See page 60.

Observation	Explanation
The colony has been restless throughout the winter. However, it has not been disturbed, it does not have poor food nor is it ill. This observation is essentially similar to that of a sick, disturbed or queenless colony. However the reasons are very different.	To begin with, the first paragraph of the observations for November should be read. On the day of the cleansing flight, study of the accumulated waste matter found on the bottom board of the hives, occupied by partially or non-selected populations, immediately reveals obvious differences. Some colonies are found where the faecal matter is covered by a thick layer of dead bees. Thick streaks of faeces between which there are dead bees and half-developed pupae lead to the conclusion that there has been an abnormally high consumption of winter provisions. Even before the day of the cleansing flight, the back window protected by a quilt is warm. Why? Because colonies which still nurse small areas of brood until December, often resume breeding in January. I have already found as early as the 15th January, brood on three frames from a hive with a strong predominance of Italian bees, which had been devastated and whose frames were scattered on the snow. As wide a surface as a hand had already been sealed. On asking the owner the value of the colony, he replied that it had never brought him any profit. Very few beekeepers are aware of this early breeding since a hive is never opened during November, December, or January. Realization of this early laying is only possible the actual day of the cleansing flight and one is not able to explain it. Many such colonies exist, at all the various stages of development, that one can think of. All crosses with Italian bees belong to this category. In the spring, these colonies lose a large number of bees which die during flight, and due to this get reinforced much later. They have a good brood in Summer, fly a great deal without ever filling up their

Observation	Explanation
	super. One can only expect a good harvest from such populations when there is plenty of honeydew, and even then they remain far behind selected populations. But even in apiaries where selection is carried out, such populations can still be found, for if they are not eliminated, their males fly several kilometers away. By using my very simple breeding method which does not require either special knowledge or equipment, any beekeeper can easily achieve this result. (See Storch. Der praktische Imker. 13th edition). To sum up: brooding until late in December and again in January is a feature inherited from the home-land of the Italian bee. In our latitude this characteristic is a drawback. What can be found on the day of the cleansing flight on the bottom board of populations not at home in our climate? Principally young bees, which having broken away from the cluster to relieve themselves, became drowsy and fall onto the bottom board to die. The others are bees that wore themselves out by caring non-stop for the brood. I have dealt at some length with this topic as it is the main reason for a poor harvest from non-selected colonies.
When, after three months of confinement, the bees leave the hive for the cleansing flight, they do not immediately fly as far away as during the honey-flow season. They face their hives and remain in this position for some time before distancing themselves tracing increasingly wider circles and then they relieve themselves.	Young bees, who a few days after their birth fly to defaecate or orientate themselves behave similarly. The same applies to bees need to re-orientate themselves on their cleansing flight because they have overwintered and been confined for a long time. This enables one to move hives or even the whole apiary, over small distances, without losing any bees, provided this is done before the cleansing flight. But beware! If, as sometimes happens, certain populations have already ventured out before the cleansing flight, moving the hives entails certain risks.
Despite being orientated in the same direction as the others the bees of certain hives fly away immediately.	Usually these colonies are already nursing a brood. The nursing bees have over-loaded bowels and are in urgent need of relief. Greater need of water! Greater food consumption!

Observation	Explanation
The bees carry the bodies of their dead into the open. They grasp a wing or a leg with their jaws and drop the body in the vicinity of the apiary.	Colonies busily clearing out the hive on the day of the cleansing flight are in order, healthy and strong. Populations that are queenless, ill or weak lack such zeal. Some have a very low mortality rate, hardly more than a hundred and such an observation must be seen as a good indication of quality. These colonies should be noted as well as those which show an increased mortality. In the latter case examination of the bottom board of the hive at the outset of the cleansing flight will provide information. Populations that are ill, develop with difficulty, and give a poor harvest every year, must be removed without hesitation. It must not be forgotten that these weaknesses are transmitted by their males. Nature practised the best form of selection in the days when sugar was not available.
Bees fall to the ground where they gather together in small clusters, running and jumping here and there.	Strong grounds for presuming the presence of latent nosema disease, or the existence of bees affected by acarine disease.
Amongst the bees scattered on the ground some have their wings arranged to look like the sail-arms of a windmill.	Very strong grounds for presuming they have acarine disease. (In both cases should be sent to the laboratory for analysis).
The hive entrance and the area in front is spread with liquid, light yellow faeces.	Acute case of nosema disease. The colony is slowly dying out. There is a great danger of the disease spreading as bees get lost or go robbing in other hives. Sulphuring must be carried out immediately.
On the day of the cleansing flight a colony fails to fly out.	First possibility: the colony feels no need to defaecate, shows a much reduced consumption of food and is healthy. In the majority of such cases the queen has not yet begun egg-laying. Experience shows that such colonies give some of the best harvests of the apiary.

Observation	Explanation
	Second possibility: during the feeding the colony was victim of an un-noticed robbing and is now in poor condition or is already dead.
	Third possibility: the colony suffocated, dying due to lack of oxygen.
	Fourth possibility: the colony over-wintered on too many frames, or did not receive enough nourishment or was not kept warm and consumed the stores in the frames upon which it overwintered. Because of persistant severe cold weather it could not move onto the other frames containing food and has died of starvation or has found itself so weak on the day of the cleansing flight that it has no strength to get out of the hive.
Bees with a swollen abdomen rush into the hive.	These are water carriers. Is the drinking place in order? These busy flights indicate several colonies are already nursing more or less large surfaces of open-brood requiring water. As egg-laying increases rapidly after the cleansing flight, the need for water increases each day.
Unfortunately, it often happens that at this time the bees can not even fly to water for several days. It is for this reason that it is advisable to give a liter of sugar solution (1/1) on the first relatively warm day.
So that this sugarwater is completely absorbed it should be given relatively hot rather than tepid and it is good to add a little liquid honey. One must take advantage of the time when the bees are found distributed between the alleys and not wait for dusk when they will be clustered together again.
Feeding on a cold March evening is completely useless and a greater part of the feeder will have to be removed the next day.

Observation	Explanation
Agitated, worried bees run on the alighting board and in front of the hive. Their special buzz (groaning) is clearly audible.	The colony has lost its queen. Not all queenless colonies are aware of their predicament the day of the cleansing flight, but from that day until the end of autumn this is the manner in which it makes its situation known in the first hours after orphanage.
One observes, especially in strong colonies, bees, as early as the day of the cleansing flight, returning to the hive with shapeless, grey, green or brownish wads.	This is not pollen, but propolis collected from the resinous buds of certain trees. These resinous scales are collected with great effort by the bees, principally from chestnut, black poplar or cherry trees.
On such a day yellow-green pollen may also be brought back.	As the bees do not yet venture far from the apiary, one can conclude that there are hazel-nut trees in the area. In certain well-protected areas, the catkins begin to be covered with pollen at the end of January. This yellow pollen may also come from sheltered snowdrops or crocus. The first pollen! Fresh hopes and dreams occupy the thoughts of the beekeeper.
A large number of bees return loaded with large wads of whitish or yellowish pollen. The origin of this pollen is a mystery.	The bees have discovered at a neighbouring beekeeper a feeder with artificial pollen.
In front of the hive lies an old, still soft queen.	If on the day of the cleansing flight the temperature is really exceptional the bees rush outside and it is not unusual for the queen to be carried along. If on the return journey she enters another hive she will be killed. When the cleansing flight is over the bees of the queenless colony run around agitated and worried and one may hear the groaning sound.

C. Spring.

Observation	Explanation
The bees carry a particularly large number of small, white sugar crystals to the hive entrance.	They are consuming stores from frames outside the nest where crystallization occurs more easily. It is advisable to give a liquid feeding immediately. The sugar solution should never be boiled or it crystallizes more easily.
In an apiary with several Carnican colonies one of the colonies has an unusually large number of Italian bees. Even during the unsettled days of March the bees from this hive fly continuously, whereas at the same time no activity takes place at the other hive entrances.	One must conclude that the colony is in the following critical situation: it has started to nurse large areas of brood too early, probably from January onwards. Such populations unaccustomed to our climate have no pollen in their frames, having consumed it during the autumn months when pollen was scarce. As for the stores of fats and albumen the bees had stocked up in their tiny bodies, these have already been used for the present brood, for nature provided nothing at that time in the season. Larvae, which should normally float in the feeding jelly can not be fed as they should and develop into bees with stunted wings and legs. Concerned for their larvae, the bees fly away to search for what is lacking but due to the cold many die on their journey. A large proportion of the bees which fly away never return. It is in this way, that colonies which have an early brood tire themselves out to the point where they put their subsistance at risk. If they survive this obstacle they only reinforce themselves during the main honey-flow and this is why their harvest is always poor. How can such populations be helped in March? By feeding them in the hive and by providing a well conserved frame containing honey and a lot of pollen.

Observation	Explanation
Each morning dead bees are found at the hive entrance, on the bottom board and in front of the hive. The bees of the colony fly around feebly and aimlessly.	This colony is definitely ill. Pay attention to the bees entering the hive at a bee-free entrance, how they come and go and eventually enter a stronger neighbouring hive. The danger of infection is great. Neighbours may get contaminated and never develop. As such a colony can never be united with another, the best solution is to sulphur it.
Small drones fly away from the hive.	At this time of the year they are the result of a queen that has not been fertilized and had already started egglaying in January, or more rarely from egg-laying workers. If an unfertilized queen is at the root of the situation, she must be removed a couple of hours before the reunion to avoid a fight, as well as the frames containing brood or eggs.
White or brownish pupae lie in front of the hive entrance. (Observations made in the early morning are more instructive, for in summer as in autumn, birds, wasps and even wind can eradicate or obscure certain signs).	This does not always signal an emergency. The larvae of the wax-moth are already at work. In their search for food these larvae upset the whole brood, hindering their development and forcing it to move upwards to the top of cells, making it impossible for the bees, to seal the brood. The resulting brood is knows as bald headed brood which is often removed from the cells. The wax-moth is a greater pest than is generally believed for it prevents hundred of bees from developing fully. If you hit an obliquely hanging frame with bald-headed brood with a hard object, this often causes several waxmoth larvae to fall out.
For several days, colonies bring in willow pollen.	During these days large pollen reserves are built up and the queen can continue to lay eggs even if bad weather were to last a long time. High consumption of winter reserves. The sooner spring pollen is brought in, the faster the colony will develop and the greater the certainty of its development. Of all the early-pollen producing trees (hazelnut, elm, etc...) the willow is the most productive. No artificial pollen can replace natural pollen.

Observation	Explanation
In the morning one observes a large amount of condensation at the hive entrance.	These colonies are already nursing large areas of brood. The amount of water found condensed at the hive entrance in the morning serves as a barometer for the egg-laying and the yield of the colonies.
A young queen (sometimes not fully developed) is found dead at the hive entrance or in front of the hive.	The old queen has been dead for a fortnight. Being queenless, the colony has bred queens and got rid of those that were superfluous. Due to the lack of males fertilization is a problem.
An old queen is found in front of the hive entrance. The population does not "lament" or appear to be in panic.	The colony has begun to breed queens on an open brood. Timely requeening in July or August often prevents major losses in the spring.
7-9° C. The bees only undertake short journeys to search for water. On such a day one colony does not fly at all.	The latter definitely has no open brood and is probably suffering misery. An emergency check-up is required. On cold April days a thorough examination at the hive entrance enables one to determine whether or not the colony has a queen.
Strewn around the hive entrance are hard, rounded wads of pollen, which often have a white coating on one side.	The bees are working on frames that have not yet held any brood and are preparing them for egg-laying. The pollen from the outer frames which is often fermented and covered with a layer of mould is removed from the cells and thrown out of the hive.
The colonies which, at the end of March and beginning of April, were restricted to a number of frames proportional to their strength, fly more vigorously than others of the same strength although the latter were left with more, albeit unused, frames.	The brood develops with greater rapidity when space remains limited, for heat is a critical factor for the timely reinforcement of the colonies. Whenever possible, populations should be kept together. Now is the time when bees should "dominate" available space. With well-confined populations, the rear window, well protected with quilts, will soon be nice and warm, whereas with those populations spread over a larger area the rear window will hardly be tepid which proves that in the latter the brood is reduced.

Observation	Explanation
	Even a small colony feels strong if kept relatively restricted. If the queen is still healthy, this is the only way to ensure complete development within time limit. What are movable frames for, if not to be used for the benefit of the colony and to our advantage?
After a risky "manipulation" within a hive, one sees a queen leaving it with her "court". This is an interesting event.	A neighbouring beekeeper of mine visited a very strong colony (at the beginning of April), and found eggs and brood from laying workers on two frames. He wished to save and use the numerous bees that were still useful at this time. He asked my advice on the matter and I told him it was only possible using a small reserve colony from a distant apiary and that special precautions would have to be taken. Each queen given to such a population would be killed and torn apart by the bees and found the following day at the hive entrance. A reserve colony from the same apiary can not be used to serve this purpose, for after having been moved, the foragers will immediately return to another hive in their former location. A small population occupying four frames, including two brood frames was placed in a transport box and taken to the apiary. Here, briefly is how we proceeded: The temperature was favourable: the morning being cool and misty, the sun broke through at about 9 o'clock. At 7.30 a.m. no hive is flying. The hive entrance to the queenless hive is closed. Scraps of felt dampered with a few drops of thyme oil were place in a swarm box with an air-grid. The strong colony was transferred to it and locked up in the swarm box. The now empty hive was thoroughly cleaned and new felt strips dampened with thyme oil placed on the bottom-board. The small population was then transferred, well restricted, within the hive. Empty spaces were filled with perfect frames full of provisions. The hive was closed. At 9 a.m. the hive entrance was opened. The bees from the small colony were quick to orientate themselves. At 10 a.m. in glorious sunshine foragers started returning loaded with pollen. At 10.30 a.m. the case containing the queenless colony

Observation	Explanation
	was opened 60 meters away from the apiary. The hampered bees, full of honey and having acquired the same odor, enter their former hive without concern and find a small population with brood of all ages. Not a single bee was wasted. My doubts concerning the queen seemed to be unfounded. Nevertheless I continued my observations, for the small colony had undergone no small amount of manipulations that day: at 7.00 a.m. transfer in the transport box, then a car journey. At 8 a.m., transferred again, into the empty hive and finally the incoming rush of honey-stuffed bees. My thoughts had been well directed, for at 11.00 a.m. the queen, a splendid specimen of Troiseck, appeared at the hive entrance. She was neither pursued or attacked by the bees, but surrounded by some fifteen workers that treated her in a friendly manner, caressing her with their antennae. She climbed along the front of the hive, was then carefully picked up and returned to the hive through the rear. I continued to watch the hive entrance for a good half-our. The queen did not show herself. I am firmly convinced that the bees which surrounded her made up her "court" as is the case when she is egg-laying. The reader can now imagine, what would have occured had I not continued my observations at the hive entrance when the operation seemed completed. Three weeks later the population was nursing five frames of brood and one was able to give the super in due time.
Bees fly, with an angled body and their legs hanging, from one hive entrance to another to get in.	These are robbers searching for, and usually finding, weak or queenless hives or hives with too large an entrance.
On certain cold days during April, or cool evenings, when the bees have long stopped flying the hive entrance of strong or even weak but well-	This is the way the bees close the hive entrance to protect their brood against the cold. At the same time they prevent the heat of the nest escaping too rapidly. The reason is the same if, on such days the following is seen: having opened the hive from behind, look at

Observation	Explanation
restricted populations is filled with clumps of bees leaving very little free space.	the bottom of the frames. You may see a barb of bees reaching to the floorboard. This is by no means a sign of there being too many young bees. This is the way they shut off the inner alleys and prevent the cold reaching the brood. Contrary to appearances, the number of bees on the brood itself may be reduced to a great extent. By placing themselves under the frames the bees protect the brood beter than if they were actually on it. This shows us that a colony will use its own vitally important heat in an economical and sensible way. (In April, the hive entrance must be kept relativity small).
Reinforced guard at the hive entrance. Isolated or general fighting.	The colony is threatened by robbers and is still defending itself. It should be helped by either reducing the hive entrance or placing a glass pane or branches in front of it. This last procedure appears to be little known.
Two of the hives within the apiary show great activity, but there is no fighting.	Robbing is at its worst. Often one of the colonies is the robber the other the robbed. In this case one permutes both colonies or immediately feeds the plundering colony. In all cases of robbing the greatest care must be exercised. If the intruding colony comes from another apiary and the victim hive has a good queen likely to develop normally, it must be kept for two or three days in a dark, calm, well-ventilated room. The first thing to do however, is to give the intruders the opportunity to escape (it is best to open the rear window of the hive at some distance from the apiary). During the next few days the victim population must be nourished and either thyme or mint oil added to the sugar syrup so as to change the smell of the hive. A sure and certain way to eliminate the danger of robbing is to move either the intruding or the victim hive at a distance of two or three kilometers from the appiary.

Observation	Explanation
The body of the robbers sometimes appears shiny and black.	These bees have lost the hairs which cover their body. This soon occurs when hundreds or thousands of bees rush greedily for the remaining honey of the victim colony. Some try to reach the supply whilst those who have filled their honey sacs try to get away. In the resulting confusion, some bees lose some of the honey harvested, which sticks in the hair of the other bees. On drying, these hairs become hard and dry and break easily. The bees also lose some of their hair by forcing themselves through narrow gaps or when fighting the guardians of the hive entrance.

Photograph 3

The main flow

During the days of the main flow one often sees a forager returning to the hive being met, even before the hive entrance, by a house bee to whom it gives the nectar which will be processed before being stored in the hive.

Photograph 4

Fanners at work

The bees do not only control the degree of humidity within the hive, but also the temperature when it is too high, by creating draughts from one to another and from the inside of the hive to the outside.
Beware! There must be no confusion between fanning for ventilation and fanning for scent-marking of the hive. In the latter case the abdomen is raised and one can see between the last two tergites a small shiny gland, the Nassonov gland, which is used to diffuse scent signals.

C. The main period of flowering.

1. May.

Observation	Explanation
Young bees with stunted wings or other malformations fall to the ground, on making their first cleansing flight.	These bees have developed from larvae having suffered from either the cold, lack of pollen or liquid nourishment and are found principally in colonies nursing a large brood. A check-up for varroasis should be carried out for this could also be the cause of malformation.
The large amount of water usually found condensed at the hive entrance in the morning is, for some colonies, greatly reduced in quantity, sometimes to a drastic extent. The same applies to flight intensity.	This is almost a sure sign of a critical situation. It is provoked by a succession of days without a harvest. One often forgets that the daily consumption of a colony with a brood is very much greater in May than April. (Immediate and copious feeding is required).
Drone pupae of varying age, are found before the hive entrance often early in the morning.	As soon as a colony has a crisis the larvae and drone pupae are the first to be sacrificed. If several very cold nights have preceded the day of this particular observation, the colony may have had to group itself in a very compact fashion and it could therefore be the brood occupying the lower portions of the frames which was inadequately protected and suffered from the cold (chilled brood).
Droplets of light yellow droppings are found on the alighting board or on the front of the hive.	May sickness is beginning. Better protection against the cold and a tepid sugar solution (1:2) or (1:3) can still prevent development of the sickness at this stage.
Young bees, with swollen and stretched abdomens, unable to defecate, fall in large number from the alighting board to the ground where they strain, in vain, to relieve themselves.	The May sickness, also called paralysis due to pollen rages. The examination of the suffering colonies shows that in most cases, they are in want of liquid nourishment. A defective insulation always promotes the development of this disease. Here also prevention is easier than curing.

Observation	Explanation
Depending on the altitude and the spring temperature, from the end of April until mid-May, there is little activity even in strong colonies and on days favorable to harvest, except perhaps during the early part of the afternoon.	This annual observation, which at low altitude occurs naturally earlier than in areas of higher altitude, is due to the fact that at this time the bees which have overwintered die quite rapidly. The bees one sees flying in the early afternoon are those young bees that will later become foragers. (From May onwards the observations made at the hive entrance must be supported by those made at the building frame).
The orientation flights of young bees are of varying intensity depending on the colony.	These flights enable one to determine with confidence the colonies that will be completely developed by the commencement of the main flow. It is not worth maintaining colonies from which one can not except a harvest. One can use their brood and their bees by sharing them between the colonies of midstrength; this should be done ten days before the main flow at the latest. This only applies to healthy colonies.
A large number of bees die suddenly. Fights take place inside the hive and at the entrance.	The bees have been poisoned by sprayed or powder insecticides.
In the morning scraps of wax are found in and in front of the hive entrance. During the day bees fly away carrying wax particles in their jaws.	The colony is breaking down worker combs to replace them by drone cells. The cappings and the parts of rotten comb are also disposed of.
Very early in the morning one finds wax-moth caterpillars in front of the hive entrance. During the day some of the bees drag wax-moth threads and cocoons onto the alighting board.	It is most likely that the bottom board was not completely cleared of wax in the spring. Amongst all this waste, the bees can only fight their bitter enemy with difficulty, for the particles of wax on which the wax-moth larvae feeds are covered by a fine cocoon.

Observation	Explanation
Healthy young bees lie dead in front of the hive entrance. Despite the fact there is a good queen, the colony is not developing normally.	This situation is not uncommon in wooded areas that are relatively warm; the cause however is seldom found. Examination of the colony reveals first a piling up of bees beneath the brood nest; some still move a little. Only on very detailed examination of the frames is the culprit found. It is the wingless female of the Mutille wasp (Mutilla Europäa). It is much the same size as a bee, with transverse bands of colour and solid jaws.
The bees return bearing on their heads two small club-shape "horns".	This occurs when the bees visit certain flowers belonging to the Orchid family. As soon as a forager, looking for nectar enters the flower, it comes into contact with two stickly pollen sacs which stick to its head. On leaving the flower the bee pulls off these two club-shaped sacs from the flower and they remain stuck to the bees head like two horns. During the flight towards another flower these horns bend down and end up at the same height as the equally sticky pistil. If they remain attached to the latter fertilization of the flower is achieved. If they do not detach themselves from the bees head the bee can then fly for whole days with these accoutrements.
Early in the morning, drowzy bees are found with their wings under the body on the alighting board.	This occurs during the honey-flow or feeding, especially in hives where the alighting board has warped or is horizontal rather than inclined downwards. Humidity condensing in the hive at night can not run off. Bees returning tumble over into the water, remain trapped and are unable to help themselves.

2. June.

Main flow. Early in the morning after a warm night a single colony is already flying, all the bees taking the same direction.	This colony has discovered, the previous evening, a source of nectar not known to the other colonies. Is it due to skill or chance? Only the harvested honey will enable one to judge this.

Crocus

Observation	Explanation
At the start of the main flow groups of bees block the hive entrance.	This situation, annoying at this time of the year, is caused by over-population. These colonies lose the inclination and dedication to work even if they are not yet affected by the swarming fever. Their inclination to work is restored by removing as soon as possible young bees and the frames containing sealed brood (formation of artificial swarms).
Blockage occurs at the hive entrances of certain colonies due to bees entering and leaving.	The hive entrance is too narrow. The fanners block it and those going out obstruct the return of heavily loaded bees. In the long run this wasting of time results in a decrease in the harvest.
Numerous pollen pellets of all colours litter the alighting board and bottom board of the hive.	The hive entrance is too narrow and its ridges too sharp. On entering the hive the bees scrape themselves and lose their pollen.
To what does one attribute the "smoothing" movements that certain of the bees make before the hive entrance?	To find the cause of these movements, which are particularly evident when the pollen harvest is plentiful, I used a magnifying glass to observe bees buzy "smoothing", without disturbing them. Only in a few cases did they continue their movements. Thanks to the magnifying glass I could ascertain that small pollen particles, invisible to the naked eye, remained attached to the bees hair. These were certainly not young bees but foragers. The colony I was watching was harvesting an unusually large amount of pollen. Whilst in other colonies I saw few or no bees "smoothing", in this one it was frequent especially when the pollen was plentiful. Finally, I concluded that the bees made these movements, which sometimes continued a long time, to rid themselves of these minute pollen grains, which slide into the gap between the head and the thorax, and can be particularly uncomfortable and annoying.

Observation	Explanation
	Although these observations are many years old I have not published them in previous editions for I doubted the exactitude of my conclusions. Recently I learnt that Dr. Karl Freudenstein had arrived at the same conclusions as myself and all my doubts have thus been removed.
All activity of a strong colony stops abruptly.	Swarming is sure to happen soon. The colony has built queen cells in which the queen has deposited eggs which may already have developed into queen larvae. These cells will soon be sealed. If one wants to prevent swarming, one must without delay cause an artificial swarm.
Between 10 and 11 a.m. you find yourself near the apiary pleased with the activity of the colonies. Suddenly you hear the sound of drones flying, which is unusual at this hour, and quickly determine from which colony they come. The colony flies irregularly and bees laden with pollen leave the hive.	This colony is going to swarm with very little delay, perhaps in a few minutes. A prime swarm usually leaves the hive as soon as the first queen cell is capped. If at this moment it is raining or the temperature is unfavourable, the colony then waits for the first fine day. In a prime swarm, the queen nearly always appears last. It builds during two weeks, not a day longer, worker cells and finally a few drone cells.
What is happening in my three reserve hives? These are empty; yet, bees fly from one to another, and some even enter these hives.	These are bees seeking a home for a swarm. Colonies ready to swarm send out their scout bees to find a shelter before the swarm departure. Once such a colony has found something suitable, it often happens that the swarm does not materialize. After having assembled in the air, it whirls around and then directly enters its new home. Empty hives should never be left open.

Observation	Explanation
Walking around the apiary in the evening when the sounds of the day are slowly dying away, one can sometimes hear a "tooting" from the hive entrance. This is a young queen in a population that has a primary swarm. The quack of the queens still in the cells is not heard so distinctly.	This colony will give the next day or at the latest on the third day a secondary swarm. In the secondary swarm, as in the prime swarm, the queen appears in front. Both leave even if the temperature is not favourable and both build only worker cells, for just under 3 weeks.
A colony that has not a prime swarm makes the well known "tooting" sound.	The queen of this colony died some two weeks ago or she was killed or wounded by a beekeeper at work, a quite frequent occurence. The next day this colony gives what one calls a prime swarm (headed by a virgin queen).
Early one afternoon, you observe your mating hives and you see a queen that wishes to enter one of them. A thin white thread (often only a small light point) is visible at the end of her abdomen. Be careful, do not stand before the hive at this moment for the queen could miss her destination.	This is the indication that the queen has been fertilized. She will begin egg-laying within the next 36 to 48 hours. But if the weather is bad or there are too few young bees, it often happens that despite abundant food, this period is prolonged. In this case one gives a little liquid honey for two or three consecutive nights. Generally the eggs then soon appear. The term fertilization is incorrect. The queen has mated. The worker egg is fertilized, not that of the drone.
The queen entering with the sign of fertilization is balled either at the hive entrance or in the mating hive. She is rarely killed.	Much has already been written about the cause of this relatively frequent occurence. But love and happiness can hardly be the reason, for a queen that arrived in an impeccable state is often in a far worse one after having been balled. One has a cripped leg, one a wing so badly damaged she can no longer fly, a third has no limbs, a fourth torn wings. Let us ask ourselves why this balling of a queen returning after fertilization happens only very rarely, if ever in a secondary swarm. Is it because in this case, the queen has, so to say grown with her swarm? Is the distribution of bees

The building-frame

Observation	Explanation
	in a secondary swarm different from that in a small mating colony? Is it the strength of this small colony which is the determining factor? There must be a reason somewhere.

Experience shows that this occurs most frequently when fertilization of the queen has been delayed by bad weather. Very often egg-laying workers develop in the mating hives and they receive the returning queen as an enemy. We also believe their appearance is due to the presence of too many old bees within the mating hives.

We have obtained the best results by building up these small colonies only with young bees taken from strong populations. These small colonies very rarely move and do not possess workers whose ovaries begin to develop. In the sealed brood of a late-fertilized queen, have you never found elongated cells from which drones emerge? The eggs from which the drones originate were laid by workers. |
| A swarm has flown and has re-entered the hive. Numerous dead bees often lie strewn before the hive entrance of a neighbouring colony. | When a swarm flies, it can sometimes happen that the queen does not follow. She may be snatched by a bird or fall to the ground in an unfavourable area where the bees can not find her. After long, fruitless searches the swarm then re-enters the hive. Bees entering the wrong hive are killed. |
| On the alighting board of strong colonies one often sees bees on the days of the main honey flow, with their tongues hanging, welcoming the foragers who return laden with honey. | The house bees are here already removing from the foragers the nectar that the latter have collected. Normally this exchange takes place within the hive. |

Observation	Explanation
On a day of main flow, there is a great deal of trafficking between the alighting boards of two neighbouring colonies; it takes place directly between the hive fronts but can also take place along more complicated routes.	Latent robbing! One colony is robbing another in the most civilized fashion. A screen placed between the hives is more often than not flown over or around. The robbers even enter the hive. This robbing is tolerated but is not satisfactory to all the colonies. Latent robbing can sometimes explain abnormally large harvests.
In warm heavy weather, clumps and barbs of bees collect from the hive. At the same time strong ventilation occurs although other activity is very weak.	When the interior temperature of the hive is too high, a large part of the colony leaves it; their instinct warns them of different dangers (softening of the combs, rupture of the combs loaded with honey or brood). If the temperature continues to rise above 36° C, the brood suffers and can die. This dead brood decomposes in the cells, but one must never confuse this with foul brood. Immediate aeration is required. This situation occurs often in hives facing south as they have no protection against the direct rays of the sun.
A few colonies assemble on the front of the hive, this even on a less hot day. A strong smell of honey emanates from the hive entrance.	The super are full. The honey is already collecting in the brood chamber of the hive. (The last two observations, like many others, may be made in July or in August depending on the temperature and altitude). As soon as possible space must be made, otherwise there is a risk of swarming or of the brood chamber becoming flooded with honey.
The bees of a secondary swarm run in all directions; on the alighting board, on the front of the hive and not uncommonly to a neighbouring colony with a good queen.	The queen has not returned from her mating flight. The swarm immediately calms down if one gives it a caged, fertilized queen. If one has a small colony with a fertilized queen, one can unite them without provoking a fight. If all else fails a frame with a capped queen cell is sufficient.

Observation	Explanation
	3. July.
Very early in the morning the bees are already returning heavily laden. Many of them rest on the alighting board or on the front of the hive, breathing deeply before entering. Those bringing back pollen are rare. At night, a strong, distinct smell of honey emanates from the hives. The bees fan more than usual and in the morning one observes that the condensed water from the hive has run onto the alighting board (inclined downwards) and has fallen to the ground.	These are almost sure signs of the appearance of honeydew, above all if, at this moment, there is no other nectar flow. The flight direction will indicate the origin of this harvest and one will soon be fixed. Very often the conifers and deciduous trees give honeydew at the same time. It is to be hoped that there is no change in the temperature. On these days cast an eye at the drinking place, the harvest barometer. One observes that it is almost empty of bees, whereas on days of no honey, it is very busy.
During a harvest of honeydew, many bees have a shiny black abdomen and waist.	Like the robbers, these bees have lost their hair and seem smaller than those which still have hair. This hair loss occurs most rapidly when the honeydew comes from pine and spruce. If one observes foragers collecting nectar on the branches of pines one can understand that they come in contact with the honeydew covered needles much more easily than when working on oak and maples. During flight, the honeydew dries, the hairs become increasingly fragile and finally fall. Beware! Do not confuse with paralysis during honeydew flow.
Badly disturbed colonies gradually cease all activity.	This is always the case when one works in the brood nest. (removal of brood frames, larvae for rearing, queen cells, etc...). The young bees stop their many activities such as feeding the open brood, fanning, keeping guard, etc... The foragers returning with pollen run anxiously on the combs, many bees visit the honey cells to fill their crops. The queen loses interest,

Helenium

Observation	Explanation
	stops egg laying and the bees stop feeding her. Several hours pass before the colony resumes its normal activity. If this happens on a day of nectar flow, these disturbances cause, as we have already mentioned elsewhere, the loss of many hundreds of grams of nectar. Beekeepers who fiddle in their colonies, often without good reason, should always keep these considerations in mind. Certain manipulations such as removing the building frames, adding frames or working without touching the nest, are not considered great disturbances which can cause bad results.
Many bees return white as if covered in flour. At the same time they bring back white pollen.	A field of poppies is within their range of activity. When the poppy flowers, the nectar flow is nearing its end, say the beekeepers of the Sudetenland, where this oleaginous plant is cultivated in an intensive way for many purposes (principally for the bakery trade). The poppy is, amongst the flowers of the garden and fields, the one that gives the most pollen. It flowers at a time when nature offers few resources. The wild poppy found in the field (corn-poppy) gives a blue-black pollen.
Artificial swarms bring back a great deal of pollen.	They are in order. It is not worth looking to see if there is a queen, as such an examination would be detrimental. These rapid flights and the intense harvesting of pollen always indicate the presence of a good queen. However, if the opposite is happening the colony must be examined without hesitation.
Bees black as coal, remarkably thin and with no hair, but capable of flying return to the colony. The number generally increases from day to day. The other bees do not appear to be hostile to them, or to push them around on the alighting board or at the hive entrance.	This colony is affected by the paralysis typical during honeydew flow (paratyphus). This disease usually breaks out between 15th of May and 15th of July. When one examines such a colony, one is often surprised at the large number of bees born in this abnormal condition. One also notices that normal bees continue to be born in the colony. Those bees and drones that are affected give the impression of being wet. Dr. Dreher has been

Photograph 5

Barbs of bees near the hive entrance

There can be various causes:
1. over-population,
2. outside temperature too high,
3. honey chamber completely full,
4. some other form of trouble.

In the first three cases, one observes many fanners at the hive entrance whilst in the last case the hive entrance is cold and empty.

Photograph 6

Expulsion of drones

Every colony with a queen expels its drones in August. The bees stop feeding these useless mouths, sometime before in order to weaken them.

Observation	Explanation
	proposing for several years, that this disease could be hereditary. Different opinions as to its causes and origins still exist. This relatively rare disease is characterized above all by the birth of black, hairless bees, which must not be confused with those that have suffered hair loss during an extended harvest of honeydew.
Bees with yellow spots on their waist enter and leave the hive.	This is pollen which has stuck to the waist. The bees become marked in this exemplary manner when they visit fields of clover or of cereals as well as the yellow toad-flax (linerea vulgaris) which flowers on rubbish dumps. I have noticed the same thing when they visit different types of compositae. These shiny yellow spots which only form slowly prove the consistency with which bees visit the same type of flowers.
When the bees have ceased flying, grey butterflies, both large and small ramble about the hive entrance.	The wax moth is searching for a place to lay its eggs and it often finds one in the gap between the alighting board and the hive, which always contains wax remains. These eggs soon become caterpillars that crawl into the hive. It is for this reason that one always finds wax moths of various ages in all the hives, even in the strong colonies that would never allow these butterflies to enter.
All the colonies fly as if in the main nectar flow, but yet the bees that return do not seem to be laden or encumbered.	The lime is flowering. It excites the bees, even when it gives no honey which is the norm. Lime trees only give honey when the water table is high and when, at the time of flowering, the weather is settled, heavy and humid.
A July storm is about to burst. Watch your bees.	Tens of thousands of bees return to the big colonies, so as not to be caught in the storm. However, this return lasts much longer than if the storm had burst at the same hour one month earlier. Why? The sources of nectar begin to dry up and so as not to return with their crops empty, many of the bees fly further a field, sometimes to a distance of several kilometres.

Observation	Explanation
	These long-distance flights do not supply much nectar for a large part is consumed as "fuel" during the flight.
If the rain lasts several days or the wind veers to the North, strong colonies have clusters of bees on the side of the hive entrance.	The old foragers, recognizable by their damaged wings and more or less bald bodies gather in this fashion at the abrupt termination of the nectar flow. They are pushed out of the colonies and will most probably not return from their next flight.
In certain of the colonies the workers begin to chase the males.	The "battle of the males" has begun. They have completed their task and are now mouths not worth feeding. All colonies chasing their drones possess a queen. Only the condition of the brood enables one to determine whether the queen herself is good enough for the next year. The best time to exchange old or worthless queens for young ones from selective breeding is now and during the month of August.
Certain colonies, sometimes all of them, remove discreetly from the hive pupae as well as young, crippled bees and carry them far away.	What strikes one on observing these evacuated bees is their stunted abdomen and the absence of one or more legs or wings. The guard bees at the hive entrance remain passive. The foragers returning to the apiary seem to have difficulty orientating themselves; robbers attempt to penetrate the hives via all the gaps. These colonies are affected by varroasis, a disease caused by a fairly large external mite (Varroa Jacobsoni). On carefully opening capped cells of male brood, on extracts the pupae and deposits them on a white sheet of paper. One can then see with the naked eye the varroas, flat, oval and of a dark brown colour (1.6 mm wide, 1.1 mm long). When the colony is infected, it is in great danger and must immediately be treated against varroasis. This find must immediately be reported to the federation or authority.

Observation	Explanation
A queenless colony with egg-laying workers is shaken at some distance from the apiary. Its bees attempts to enter neighbouring colonies that have good queens.	The shaken bees first fly towards their old hive. Finding it shut they place themselves near the hive entrance. Soon "emissaries" direct themselves towards the alighting boards of neighbouring colonies, which as in times of robbery, have reinforced the guards. It then seems as if a dialogue between the two parties is established for their antennae move avidly. The petitioners lie on the wood, as if to imply that they do not wish to fight. When their peaceful intensions are recognized and after a strict examination entry is allowed. If before shaking the bees they are given the opportunity to fill their crops with honey, entry is made without a fight and with greater speed. This confirms that, when the bees are sated and encumbered many "operations" are more easily achieved. One must attribute no great value to such reinforcements and none at all if they take place after 15th August, when the nectar flow has ended, for nearly all the bees are old and will soon die. If the colony has a drone-laying queen, she must be removed several hours before the operation. If one wishes to avoid pointless fights the shaken bees must feel orphaned when they seek admittance to other colonies. A full crop is not always enough.

Geranium

E. The drawing in of winter.

1. August.

Observation	Explanation
Stimulative feeding was already provided for 10 to 12 days in July. Compare the flight activity and quantity of pollen returned by the colonies that were fed with the much reduced activity of colonies, which, as an experiment, had not been fed.	By feeding (1:1) the colony, we are cheating it by providing it with a nectar flow. As experience has shown the addition of a little honey gives even better results. The numerous larvae demand extra care from the old foragers. The numerous flights involved in effect purify the colony by eliminating those bees that could otherwise have fallen ill and littered the bottom board. It is in this way that one creates a strong strain of bees ready to overwinter.
At what time of the year should the colonies no longer have any brood?	The majority of beekeepers do not realize to what a great extent the value of a colony or of a particular race or breed can be increased in our regions by the timely termination of egg laying. Observations made and compared, over a period of years enable one to draw conclusions confirming this. Why does the native bee survive the winter so well? Why does it consume so little of its stores and have such a low mortality rate? Why does it greet the spring in such a fit condition with stores that are hardly touched? Because the latter are not used to feed useless late brood and because, well adapted to our climatic conditions, the native bee ceases to lay eggs as soon as the sources of nectar and pollen in the fields dry up. I have raised these bees in the area of the Sudetenland. As early as the end of August there were no longer any eggs in the majority of the colonies. Nowadays the native bee is often replaced by the gentle Carniolan types "Peschets", "Troiseck", or "Sklemar" which originate from the eastern Alps. Sometimes beekeepers complain that this bee abruptly ceases to lay eggs in August and does not even let itself be influenced by stimulative feeding. If the queen continues to lay, the bees remove the eggs from the cells. They behave in this respect, exactly like those bees that formerly used to inhabit the hol-

Observation	Explanation
	low trees of our old forests. It is for this reason that they overwinter just as well as our native bees. One should not complain of this end to the laying of eggs but, on the contrary, should rejoice, for it is the only reason why a colony can enclose itself within a winter cluster with bees that are not worn out. This race of bees that is well suited for the Spring harvest and which gives one no cause for complaint has replaced the native race that was spurious and unproductive. What would have become of beekeeping if one had not discovered the Carniolan breed? I can only recommend the more widespread use of this race by all beekeepers. I have shown how this is possible with my very simple procedure for the breeding of queens. (see Storch »Der praktische Imker«).
A group of weakened drones is found in the area of the hive entrance.	The "battle" of the males is nearing its end. In a few days they shall all be dead in front of the hive. One should realize that nature did well not to supply weapons to the drones!
At very nearly the same time several colonies remove drone pupae that are white, brown and almost fully developed to the hive entrance.	The last brood of drones still in the colony is being removed from the cells. (This can also occur in July). Colonies which have a strong tendency for egg-laying, generally remove the drone larvae a few days later than the others.
A colony still tolerates the presence of drones. There is a large number of bees keeping guard at the hive entrance and they examine every bee meticulously before allowing it to enter the hive. They fly rather weakly but the departures and returns of the foragers are rapid and certain. They bring in a great deal of pollen.	It is most likely that this colony is changing its queen. In this case it will possess up to 3 maternal queen cells or already have a recently born young queen. The colony will retain its males for prospective mating. Such colonies usually have large stores of honey and pollen. The queens that come from such a colony are often very valuable. A brief examination of the colony will enable one to ascertain the most probable mating date. By placing a distinctive mark near the hive entrance one facilitates the queen's re-entry. In this case, it is not unusual to find the old

Observation	Explanation
	queen continuing to lay eggs whilst the young queen begins. One day however one will find the old queen dead in front of the hive entrance, often still surrounded by a few bees.
A colony has not yet chased away its drones; it flies very feebly even on the days of main flow. A few bees fly alone and without much conviction and seem to hesitate before entering the hive. Very few return with pollen.	This colony has no queen and no possibility of raising a new one. It does not appear to have any laying workers yet, for then flight would be more intense. One can not let a colony remain in this condition. Because of the lateness of the season, union is preferable to requeening. The surplus pollen frames are shared between the hives.
An artificial swarm with a queen from that year seems to be perfectly in order but flies feebly.	Upon examination one finds only two to three frames with brood and a lack of nurse bees. This is too few for successful overwintering and normal spring development. The colony must progressively be strengthened by giving single frames of brood, without bees, from a strong colony, or by uniting the weak colony with another swarm.
After mating and until the following summer, a queen with markings produces uniformly grey bees, like Carniolans. Following this, a large number of bees with one or two coloured tergites are produced.	The queen has been fertilized by at least two drones of different breeds. Although suspected for a long time, since the summer of 1953 we know for certain that queens fertilized more than once are the rule, rather than the exception.
A sour smell of rot and strong glue escapes from the hive entrance of a colony. In front of the entrance or in the gap between the hive and the alighting board one observes small dark brown spheres the size of a pinhead.	The brood of this colony is sick. On opening the hive the bad smell becomes even more pronounced. To begin with, one examines the frames with recent brood to see whether the capped cells are collapsed or perforated. If these cells contain a viscous liquid that one can draw out into a thread by means of a small stick, this colony is affected by American or malignant foul brood. If it were European or benign foul

Observation	Explanation
	brood the cell contents would not be viscous. In both cases the dead brood is more often than not dehydrated and has the shape of brown scales adhering to the inner cell walls. These extremely contagious diseases must be reported to the authorities.
On a day of main flow one colony has not a single fanner near the hive entrance. In the morning the latter is absolutely dry. Concurrently one observes strong colonies forming barbs before the hive (starvation barb). The bees still fly but do so feebly and aimlessly.	This colony is suffering from extreme starvation. It has already absorbed the jelly of all the open brood. There are no longer any larvae. The capped brood begins to cool. If one does not feed immediately, it will not fly at all on the following day. Chilling of the brood will follow, many bees will fall to the bottom board of the hive, hundreds of others will die in the cells and the queen will die last of all. This situation can arise when there have been several days without a harvest or when one removes too much honey from colonies that lay a great many eggs. Even in August, a colony must be able to draw from plentiful supplies. Why?
Certain colonies reduce their hive entrance by means of a curtain of propolis only leaving a small opening the size of a thumb.	This occurs when the hive entrance is either too wide or too high. A colony which does this to prevent the wind and cold penetrating the hive in winter is not very strong.
The colonies are tormented by wasps. Fights take place at the hive entrance.	Some years, the wasps are so numerous that they seriously affect the harvest on days of main flow. One must set up wasps traps. Hundreds per day can be caught in a feeding flask containing beer or diluted fruit juice. Wasps are also attracted to the hive if the dead bees in front of it are not regularly removed.
Robbers attempt to slip inside the hive, sometimes in a very crafty manner. The alighting boards are then well occupied by guardian bees.	The danger posed by robbery is far greater in August than in April. Many foragers still attempt to bring something back before dying. One must reduce the size of the hive entrance in time, in proportion to the strength of the colony. The robbers are surprisingly

Observation	Explanation
	stubborn. They manage to slip through a 3 mm gap, or a key hole to find a pot of honey combs kept in a hive or cupboard that is not properly sealed. Once a queenless colony is liquidated or no longer defends itself, the robbers will attack other hives or even a neighbouring apiary. All robbery originates from some negligence or omission. Ignorance is often the reason for the great losses due to robbery.
	Here is an example meant as a warning! About mid-August, while the beekeeper was away, his wife had placed the extractor, a container with cappings and a few frames still moist with a smearing of honey in front of the hives. She believed that the job of cleaning would only occupy the bees of her own apiary. Catastrophe! Tens of thousands of bees arrived from all directions and when all had been cleaned off the extractor and frames, they attacked the colonies, which, with the exception of two, courageously defended themselves and could still be saved by the beekeeper. For several days in succession, his colonies as well as those of the neighbouring apiaries were greatly inconvenienced by the robbers.

2. September.

Observation	Explanation
A hum of wings like the sound of an engine can be heard day and night during feeding. The fanners are well distributed, right up to the front, on the whole surface of the alighting board.	The excess water contained in the food is being removed from the hives. This means a great deal of work for each colony. The more dilute the solution, the longer this task will last. Within the hive numerous bees fan and chase the warm, humid air towards the fanners at the hive entrance. It is perferable to feed with concentrated solutions (3:2). For many reasons the feeding should be finished by 10th September.
There is a great deal of traffic between the hive entrances of two of the colonies during the feeding.	The bees of one colony are penetrating the neighbouring one and returning, their crops stuffed with honey. This case is analogous to that of the latent robbing observed during main flow.

Observation	Explanation
On a warm sunny day in September, usually about mid-day, one observes many bees flying but their movements are relatively limited.	The last bees born in August or later are relieving themselves and making their orientation flights. If these flights are intense, the winter clusters will be large and these colonies will have a greater resistance against possible dangers until the following spring. Except in those regions providing a late plentiful nectar flow, one must never omit the stimulative feeding in August.
Even though the feeding has ended, certain colonies still bring in a lot of pollen.	These colonies, stimulated by the feeding, still have large surfaces of brood whose great needs are catered for, from the winter stores. It is advisable to compensate for this loss, in October, by an additional feeding. However, do not be over-generous for the cells must remain empty for the winter cluster.

3. October.

Observation	Explanation
The number of orientation and cleansing flights diminishes progressively from day to day. Certain colonies do not fly at all from mid-October.	These colonies no longer have any open brood. If they still have capped cells, they are few in number and the births are imminent. If the winter rest goes undisturbed, the queens will only resume egg laying when the sun is again high in the sky. One of the principal conditions for a good overwintering is thus fulfilled.
All the colonies within the apiary have a great deal of humidity at the hive entrance, even during the last fortnight of October.	The feeding has been prolonged through until October even though the necessary sugar was available in August. To justify this, the pretext is often made that when feeding is stopped before September, the colonies waste their winter stores on feeding the brood. Why does late feeding constitute an error? Because it implies one has forgotten that the colony has already prepared itself for overwintering. It has already got rid of the majority of the old foragers. The bees that remain must carry out this extra work and will lose their full potential for spring development.

Observation	Explanation
	Consider the following: fifteen pounds of sugar in a solution of 3:2 (3 parts of sugar for 2 of water) gives exactly ten liters of solution. This is equivalent to a bucket full to the brim. Despite the lateness of the season, this enormous quantity must not only be absorbed and stored by the colony but be concentrated and capped by the bees after they have added different ferments to it. All this work is asked of them just before the onset of winter and despite this, one hopes for a good spring development of these colonies. There are several other reasons why late feeding is wrong, it can even provoke an outbreak of nosema.
Even when the colonies are healthy, the expulsion of many bees from the hive begins at the end of August and lasts until mid-October. Those that are expelled do not crawl or jump around and do not have swollen abdomens.	It is not often that once reads about this behaviour which recurs every year. Some call it, with good reason, the battle of the workers, comparing it with the battle of the males which occurs when colonies with a good queen chase away their drones. During these weeks, the colonies will slowly reject the old foragers, worn out by harvesting and caring for the brood. Indeed the majority of them undertake a last excursion and die in the fields; those found in front of the hive represent only a small fraction. What can be the deep-rooted cause for the death of so many bees, amongst which are many still capable of flying? The reason is that which will be able to work on the colony's development the following spring, that is, those bees not worn out. Such colonies have few deaths at the end of the winter, have a quiet winter and have the inherited instinct to stop brooding as soon as nature no longer provides nourishment. In our apiaries, there are still many colonies, principally those crossed with Italian bees that still do not have this primordial quality resulting in good harvests.
At the temperature of 5° C, when not a single bee flies, one sees wasps entering and leaving the hives undisturbed.	They are eating the provisions found in the frames not occupied by the bees. If one squashes one leaving the hive, one finds evidence of this theft (wasps-traps are still effective at this time. They must be placed in the sun and the contents shaken so that the smell spreads and attracts the robbers).

Photograph 7

Robbery

When a colony is greatly troubled by robbers and continues to defend itself, it is sufficient to place before the hive entrance, previously reduced to the width of a finger, a few leafy twigs. This means of protection proves far more effective than a pane of glass positioned in the same place.

Photograph 8

Protection of the hive entrance

During the winter months, beekeepers protect their colonies against the wind as well as the sun in many different ways. The above photograph shows a hive bearing a characteristic decoration and an entrance protected by a plank with a small opening for the purpose of aeration.

Observation	Explanation
	4. November.
If in November there are still a few days of good weather some colonies make the most of this opportunity to bring in a lot of pollen.	Examination of such colonies, that I have always carried out with the permission of the owners concerned, has revealed each time not only the presence of capped and open brood but also the presence of eggs. Whilst I have already warned in chapter A (during the Winter) of the really disastrous consequences of such late egg-laying in our latitudes. I would like here to relate one of the main reasons why such colonies always have a bad winter. Everyone knows that a few days after their birth the young bees must rid themselves of the waste-matter still in their bowels. But this brood still open in November, whose normal place is at the heart of the colony, will produce bees that will not have the opportunity to go out on their cleansing flight. On trying to leave the cluster they continually upset the population in its winter rest. A few manage to fly away and die in the snow, or else fall, drowzy, onto the bottom of the hive. All the colonies that we examined and where we made the above observations have revealed themselves as being a cross with Italian bees. This fact should provoke thought and corrective action.
A warm, sunny day follow a spell of cold, wet weather. The bees of every colony fly actively. In front of one of the hives one observes several that crawl and jump but don't manage to fly.	Great attention must be paid to this observation, which can also be made during the preceding months after the end of the flights, for these are probably bees affected by acarine. Only examination by microscope can determine the disease precisely.

Observation	Explanation
On late but favourable flying days, the bees behave as if spring were near. They fly noisily and circle the apiary, before being forced to endure several months of confinement in the obscurity of the hive.	Every beekeeper will rejoice at these late flights from which those old bees that are worn out or ill will not return. Every colony acclimatised to our latitudes will only shelter those bees that will permit normal development in the spring. The young bees just recently born have the opportunity to defecate and the bottom board of the hive will be clean for the last dead bees will have been removed from the hive. Soon the outside temperature, in the day as well as at night, drops from day to day. Our bees group themselves to form the winter cluster. Warmly protected and well cared for by the beekeeper they will lie dormant until the following spring.

F. The winter bottom board cover.

During the winter months each colony writes its history on the bottom board of its hive (or on the board cover that one slides beneath the frames at the onset of winter). This history can vary a great deal from one population to another and enables the beekeeper to draw conclusions as to the health or well-being and the future development of his bees. The summary below provides a valuable complement to the observations made at the hive entrance. The most profitable time for this cover to be removed, so that the best observations can be made, is at the beginning of the cleansing flight. It is worth noting the observations on the hives identity card.

Observation	Explanation
4 to 5 bands of decay on the bottom board, those in the centre are longer than the other; the overall outline being elliptical.	A healthy colony strong and promising. Even those with only 3 or 4 bands of decay can be classed amongst the strong colonies.
A few dead bees lie scattered amongst the bands of decay, that is, just beneath the winter cluster.	This colony is healthy and its winter rest went undisturbed.
Those bees that died during the winter are scattered all over the bottom board. Some have their legs wide-spread.	These are bees that have fallen drowsy from the cluster onto the bottom board after being disturbed (by tits, wind, etc...).
Amongst the decay there are eggs and white or brownish worker pupae.	The colony is in order. The queen has already been egg laying for a considerable time. Wax-moth caterpillars are probably at work.
Dwarf drone pupae are found on or between the bands of faeces.	A virgin queen or egg laying workers have already been egg laying for a considerable length of time.

Observation	Explanation
The bands of decay are incredibly thin and shallow.	An economical colony; it does not yet have any brood and has overwintered perfectly.
The bands of decay are brownish in colour.	The combs are very old.
In some of the beeways between combs there is as yet no decay.	The colony must be soon contracted tightly together (to economize on heat).
The bands of decay are all the same length as the free beeways.	The colony is too contracted; there is a danger of too high a consumption, enlarge the colony soon by giving frames full of stores.
A dead queen is amongst the dead bees.	The colony is queenless. If when the queen died she had already begun egg laying, the colony probably has a queen yet she will not be fertilized for there are no drones.
Numerous white crystals are to be found between and near the decay.	The winter stores have crystallized. A liquid feed must be given without delay otherwise the bees will soon suffer from the lack of water.
The decay bands are all on one side of the hive and are arranged in a semi-circle.	In search of warmth, the colony has clung to one of the party walls with another population to form a single cluster.

Observation	Explanation
Amongst the winter decay one finds isolated or numerous varroas corpses.	The stand colonies are all, more or less, affected by varroasis. Taking the most favourable case and multiplying the number of corpses found by twenty, one can evaluate the number of varroas still living in the hive. But if the number of corpses is very great one must multiply the number by eighty. After the cleansing flight, all the colonies must be treated. This find must be reported to the federation or competent authorities.
A quantity of dead bees on the bottom board sometimes forming a layer the thickness of a finger.	Strong likelyhood of disease; nosema, acarine; or else the colony is beginning egg laying very early.
The colony has died beneath its stores.	The colony was seriously affected by acarine or it suffocated due to lack of oxygen.
The colony has died beside its stores.	The colony had consumed all the stores that were in the combs of the winter cluster, at the onset of extreme cold it was unable to move itself to those frames still containing stores.

G. The building-frame.

Mr PASCHKE, the inventor of the building frame, had originally called it the hive barometer, nothing to do with the temperature of course! Next, he called it the window to watch and finally the building frame (Baurahmen). In effect, it is all of these things at the same time. Whatever one calls it, its main purpose is to inform us of what is happening within the hive, without having to visit the colony. But to watch alone is not sufficient, one must understand what one sees. Nowadays the building frame, which in its early days was strongly critized by many specialists of the beekeeping fraternity, has gained acceptance, not only in Germany but in many other areas, for those who use it do not wish to do without it. The information it provides is not only valuable but enjoyable. Is it not pleasing to be able to observe the queen and her court, to watch her laying eggs, the bees' dance and the development of the brood? It is for this reason we thought these observations admirably complement those made at the hive entrance and from the board cover, the more so as any hive can easily be fitted with such a window.

In winter.

The glass pane of the window is arranged facing towards the inside of the hive and the free space filled with corrugated paper for insulation.

Observation	Explanation
The winter cluster is drawn tightly together.	The colony is in order and will overwinter without problems.
The colony is not quiet and makes continuous murmur.	The colony is in need of air. Check that the hive entrance is not blocked.
One finds faeces on the window pane and the bees are agitated.	The beginning of an attack of dysentery. The population must be removed even if the weather is cold and the queen sought out. If one does not find her the colony must be sulphured.
If dysentery only breaks out in March.	The hive can still be saved. From the very first days of flight a syrup flavoured with honey must be administered.

Observation	Explanation
There are traces of humidity on the window pane.	The insulation is inadequate and must be improved immediately.

In spring and summer.

After the cleansing flight the window must be reversed, the building frame is positioned with a starter strip of comb foundation, and then the window-glass outside. Usually after this operation one is settled until the end of summer, except of course for the periodic removal of the building frame which must be cut once a week, even if it is not fully built up. The operation only takes a couple of minutes and is not upsetting for the colony.

Observation	Explanation
A colony is not working at the building frame.	The colony is not in order. One must check whether there is a queen and a sufficient quantity of bees. The colony can eventually be strengthened with bees found on the building frame of well populated hives.
The colony builds up its building frame within a week.	All is in order. One must enlarge the colonies that have built up the building frame in a week or less.
The work on the building frame has ceased in all of the colonies.	Either it is raining or it is a time with no nectar flow.
A single colony ceases to work on the building frame.	Swarming fever is affecting the colony.

Observation	Explanation
A colony has built only a small heartshape at the building frame with acorn cups at the bottom.	A sure sign of swarming, which will take place in about a fortnight's time - or the colony is queenless.
The edges of the building frame cells are very much thicker than usual.	There are not enough frames in the hive. A foundation frame should be given.
The colony builds up its building frame entirely with worker cells.	There is no longer any danger of swarming for this particular year or else the queen has been replaced without swarming.
Bees are building combs everywhere paying no attention to the building frame foundation.	The building frame has been badly replaced and the distance between it and the frames of the brood nest is greater than 10 mm.
The bees have withdrawn from the window and occupy the beeways at the bottom of the frames.	The beekeeper has made an error. The glass pane of the window has been badly replaced and lets air in or the pane is too thin and allows heat to escape.
The colony is building wax nets on the window pane of the building frame.	This is a good quality colony.
A colony changes quickly from building combs of large cells to building combs of worker cells.	This is a quality colony and it will not have swarming fever.
The building frame is built up in a single day and is completely filled with eggs.	Main flow. There is no longer any room in the brood nest to satisfy the egg laying queen, wax foundations should be given otherwise there is risk of swarming.

Observation	Explanation
The building frame is built up in a single day and is full of liquid honey.	Main flow; remove that which is capped, give one or more frames of foundation otherwise there is risk of swarming.
Agitation (running around) on the window of the building frame.	The first few hours of queenlessness. Look at the hive entrance; the bees are agitated and appear to be looking for something.
Males are present at the building frame window.	They have become useless and will soon be chased from the hive.
Although there is no starter strip of comb foundation, the bees begin to build worker cells.	This comb must not be cut, one must wait for it to be full of honey and capped. Use it as honey comb. It could be that this is a prime swarm headed by a virgin queen.

Conclusion.

Many wish to become beekeepers having no previous knowledge of the field. This usually happens in the following manner: one builds an apiary, buys all the gear, hives, colonies, swarms; one spends a great deal of money and begins beekeeping without at the same time deepening one's knowledge within this field.

And despite this one hopes for success.

But apiculture is not an occupation where one can permit oneself to act in that way without paying dearly for it. For as long as the hive hides only mysteries, for as long as he cannot understand the events, not knowing the causes or consequences, as long as he can not realize and understand the relationship that exist between nature and the hive, his harvests will not and cannot be anything but very modest or else they will be due to luck alone.

Idealism is all very well - I would be the last person to underestimate its importance - but is is most unwise to approach beekeeping in this way. One should try to make the best of any enterprise.

Furthermore, from where does the idealism of these beekeepers, who remain rooted in ignorance come from? In their hands, the colonies have to endure all sorts of torment and suffering throughout the year and even often misery and death.

Only one who has read and studied knows how to protect them against all these errors, he alone can determine the care which the colony needs for its well being, only he is capable of working in accordance with local conditions and using them to the best advantage of his colonies, for their development and the maintenance of their activity.

It is all this which makes for success.

The observations discussed in this current work will help the beekeeper enormously in learning to recognize, understand and interpret the different situations presented by the apiary. The beekeeper will only be worthy of the title the day a look at the hive entrance and another at the rear window or beneath the frames tells him with certainty the internal situation of the colony.

H. STORCH.

Everything for the beekeeper

16 HIVES PATTERNS AND MODELS:
mounted or not.

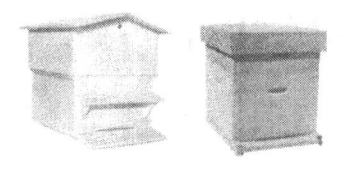

ALL THE BEST WOOD:
high altitude spruce-tree; slow growth hence lasting; light despite a 25 mm thickness; good natural insulator.

ALL THE BEST QUALITY MADE PRODUCTS:
the most rigid assembling (with assembly studs) for the framework and the supers as well as for the fast-assembling frames (the frames interlock without nails, glues, nor clamps).

ALL THE STAINLESS STEEL BEEKEEPING EQUIPMENT
47 types of extractors.

36, 38 rue du Commerce
74200 THONON LES BAINS
Haute Savoie - France
tél. (50) 71.03.22
télex 385417

MAX MENTHON

Efficiency • Resistance • Competivity

E.H. THORNE *(Beehives)* LTD

Registered Office:
BEEHIVE WORKS - WRAGBY - LINCOLN LN3 5LA
TELEPHONE: WRAGBY (0673) 858555

When you buy the best,
you not only get a better article,
you get it quicker &
you are fully satisfied.

Robert Lee (bee supplies) Ltd

Sole UK distributors of Ets THOMAS quality honey processing plant

For all yours beekeeping equipment

HELPFULL   FRIENDLY   DEPENDABLE

the finest equipment
the largest selection
the best value for money

FREE CATALOGUE ON REQUEST

High Street, Cowley, UXBRIDGE, Middlesex UB8 2BB
Telephone: UXBRIDGE (0895) 33181 & 35727

Made in the USA
Columbia, SC
28 August 2017